54
Golden
Pieces

54 Golden Pieces

Copyright © 2023 by Jean René Bazin PierrePierre. All rights reserved.

No part of this publication may be reproduced, stored in a retrieval system, or transmitted in any form or by any means, digital, electronic, mechanical, photocopying, recording, or otherwise, or conveyed via the Internet or a website without prior written permission of the publisher, except in the case of brief quotations embodied in critical articles and reviews.

All illustrations by the Haitian artist Patrick Gaspard.

ISBN: 979-8-9892304-1-9 (hardcover)
        979-8-9892304-0-2 (paperback)
        979-8-9892304-2-6 (ebook)

Printed in the United States of America

54
Golden
Pieces

Jean René Bazin PierrePierre

Table of Contents

Preamble ix

Opportunity. 1
The Pillow 2
The Girl I Love. 3
Birthday Wishes 4
Come Home 5
The Wrap (I). 7
The Wrap (II) 9
Planeful Of Inmates 12
Lost Love 16
Unfinished... 17
To My Dear Friend. 18
To My Baby 19
Say. 20
Morning Plight. 21
Frankly Speaking 22
Despair. 23
The Gift 24
Loud And Clear 25
Did I Miss You. 26
Life Without You 27
Crosses And Clay 29
I'll Walk Away 30
One Of These Days 31
Loving You. 32
Say It 33
Father. 34
Your Spell. 35

Come	36
To You Again	37
Sudden Voyage	38
Love's Coin	39
Mahogany Queen	41
My Oath	42
When She Calls	43
Surrender	45
Flight From The City	46
Been a While	48
Our Eyes	50
The Spark	51
The Bliss	52
I Could	53
The Bug	54
Speak To Me Softly	56
At Stranger	58
Of This World	59
Darkest Hour	60
With A Gift	61
My Lovely Little Bird	62
None Else More	64
"What Is This?"	66
Sweeter Than You	67
Sing Alleluia	68
Hurry	70
To You	71
Rhyming	74
Their Plight	76
The Love Of God	78
Sheer Clemency	79

My Treat	80
Nothing	81
Your Face	82
Tobago, Damn!	83
Nighterie	85
One Day	86
Listen	87
The Right Time	88
Generescence	90
Your Eyes	92
God's Love	93
Intuition	94
Nursing	96
Sometimes	97
Mirage	98
When They're Gone	99
Don't Shed Tears	101
A Lovely Day	102
My Abducted Child	103
Deep In Her Soul	106
O Lord	108
Mighty Deeds	109
Souvenirs	111
Dear Lord	112
Blessed Assurance	113
Were It Not	114
Dear Father	116
To My Baby	117
First Kiss	119
Once We Had	121
Peace And Love	122

I Always Wonder	123
Damned Sunrise	125
Sheer Unison	126
My Flat	128
Your Heart	129
Daydream At The Gym	131
If One Day	132
Brand New	133
Dreamy Whisper	135
Nowatimes	136

Preamble

— In this great City of ours, capital of the world as it is often named, we are millions over millions of souls mingling with one another. For these interactions to occur more or less smoothly, great minds got together and set up rules and regulations. They exist to protect the right and safety of each and every soul living in the City.
When anyone infringes these rules, penalties voted adequate and fitted are applied. But if these violations or transgressions result in bodily injuries of another living soul, the penalties are much more severe.
— In this universe of ours, created lovingly by our Almighty Father, He set up rules and regulations designed to keep all His children safe from harm. He repeatedly sent messengers to recall us of these rules. Then, out of love, He came down Himself to ensure that we adhere to these basic rules upon which the world foundation rests.
— Picture the chaos that would become the City if everyone were to decide not to stop at red lights and stop sign.
— Picture, therefore, just as much peaceful the world would be if the spiritual directives given from its creation were uphold and applied... Just picture!!!

Opportunity

He comes early morning to deliver the news
She opens up the door and feels the morning dew

He, just like other days, ignores that she exists
She attempts desperately to stay calm, bites her fist

He thinks that hopefully one day he'll buy this house
She shakes repeatedly the dried up summer blouse

He suddenly sees her. How lovely, is his thought
She startled quite lightly, greeting word she found naught

He waves at her shyly, and "howdy" he utters
She still says not a word, clinging to the shutters

You could feel the second stalling the next instant
Trying to set the stage to their muffled intent

But time waits for no one and before you next breath
The occasion offered is put back on its shelf

Hoping for the next morn that may just never show
She returns to her chores, hugging back her sorrow

He returns to his route, trying to stow away
The thoughts that for now on will warm him on his way

The Pillow

This pillow that I hug so tight
Recalls your scent of our last night.
My lonely heart skipping a beat
Misses sadly its lovely treat
And this nightmare of your absence
Comes back to me as cruel nuisance.

Then quietly my mind evades
To a land of much lovely shades,
That dreamland where you reign as queen
Where I can bathe in sweeter scenes…
And the pillow watching the show,
Applauds when hand in hand we go.

The Girl I Love

One of these mornings I woke up,
Tired, weary and all fed up
Of the continual happenings
That trouble us, all living things.
So I nonchalantly got up,
Looking for what could cheer me up.
Gently on my thinker, sweet dove,
Gently came perch the girl I love.

She's no goddess, no cover girl
But nonetheless makes my heart swirl.
She's no Marylyn, no angel
But my mixed feelings, unravels.
She brings to me the light of day.
Her face I see each time I pray.
Whether sent by Zeus, God or Jove,
I still treasure the girl I love.

So through my life I go daily,
Some happily, some painfully
But deep in her brown eyes gazing,
I feel I can do anything.
I can be blessed with solid health
Or rewarded with lasting wealth
But from all gifts sent from above
The best by far's the girl I love.

Birthday Wishes

Why are people driven towards one another,
Remains a mystery.
But whether to stifle the feel or to utter
Can be a misery.

To confide or not to
My sweet tickle for you
Is the plight I carry
While wishing you're happy!

Come Home

Come home to me,
Let's end this misery.
Come home to me
Let's work at being happy.

The days drag without you into senseless evenings
And even old Trixie will not lick its pudding,
The flowers faded away
And the grass has turned to gray
And the squirrel gave up its early day begging.

Come home to me
I never meant to say,
Come home to me
The words you heard that day

They were only mere thoughts of a deep troubled mind
Expressing the sorrow of a past left behind.
To who's bitten and twice shy,
All is first seen as a lie
And just disconcerting when honesty he finds.

Come home to me,
Come bring life to my world
And you will see
The way I treat a pearl.

For the bedroom mirror misses your reflection.
It looks much lovelier bringing your description,
Either your eyes of pure jade,
Your many dancing parades
Or your modeling spree done with verbal caption.

Come home to me
Come and get back your baby,
Come home to me,
Let us work at being three.

The Wrap (I)

To every man upon this earth
Is attached a soul mate at birth.
This truth remains on solid ground
Whether it makes you smile or frown.

So all through this life we then go
Accompanied by a shadow
We often ignore but, helas!
One blasted day they show their class.

The relation between each pair
At times can be much more than fair
But yet for some unknown reason
One can be trapped in a prison.

What to many can be merry,
To others can be misery
And one wonders, in honesty,
Why such dissimilarity.

So in the same block of a street
Some of us lose, others profit.
Don't go too far to understand,
The clue is much closer at hand.

This shadow, the alter ego,
Often is source of your sorrow
Mostly when the plans it upholds
Brings only trouble but no gold.

Therefore you live on their behalf
Craving for what the others have
While selfishly they go pursue
Their goals while you remained subdued.

The Wrap (II)

I will forever be your mate,
Upon the earth this is your fate
We'll go together hand in hand
Through this life, till the very end.

To understand this old decree
You will have to cross the deep sea
That separate earthly matter
From the most infinite ether.

Way before the start of your time
We were singing with lovely rhyme.
Our souls woven in harmony
Would always do great euphony.

But then one day you chose to leave,
Forsaking all we had received
For some unknown destination,
For some brand new constellation.

I drifted away aimlessly,
Searching for you so desperately
For a long time I could not find
That blissful peace you left behind.

After light years of misery,
After much frantic inquiry
I came to conclude bitterly
To think of you posthumously.

Then one day I felt your aura
Upon the rays of Aurora
Who brought me one early morning
Your sorrow and your suffering.

There I followed you in your pain,
Was there when finally it end'
And sadly watched you go again
Step right into your lion's den.

You always in your suffering,
Equally to me sorrow bring.
And every drop of tears you shed
Brought the amount of blood I bled.

It lasted month, then came the years
But time did not palliate my fears.
I dreaded each of your affairs
And pitied more the vows you shared

Then I decided that you should
Stay alone as much as you could,
This way we can regain the bliss
And as before enjoy our peace.

I found a way to discourage
Your heart so you can turn the page
On whoever could your heart please,
On your swings of love put a freeze.

I brought you lasting, treasured things
As sign of my love offering
But since others it'd benefit
I retained these spiritual treats.

And silently I will remain
Around you so you understand
That after all is said and done
Between us there should be no one.

Planeful Of Inmates

On a lovely spring day,
Two years ago, this May,
A plane full of inmates
Departed from the States.

They boarded all weary
Though for some, the journey
Was the first in lifetime;
They knew that was no prime.

So they boarded in pair
Two by two in the air
Willing to see whether
They could go wherever.

Some dreamed of a plane crash
While others saw a bash
That would last three hours
While they won't be ours.

But little did they know
That on their way to go,
Nature and all its friends
Their journey would soon end.

So they laughed and they sang
So loud the captain rang
The seatbelt sign over
And over the speaker.

And then they departed,
Happy and elated
To be so far away
From their cells for one day.

The plan was they would go
Straight up to Key Largo,
Work the ground, as they should,
Leave as soon as they could.

But next to Key Largo
They are islands to go.
With determination
You'll find new horizons.

Nature in the tropics
Has a touch of epics.
You never, never know
From where the next wing blows.

So when just suddenly
The rain fell profusely,
The clouds around the sun
Edge to the guards gave none

And the shadows falling
And the big trees helping
Gave way, mongst other things,
Big breaks for escaping.

Said it was a sure thing,
Later in broadcasting;
Taken by swift surprise
The guards were done by size.

They were found in shackle,
Pitiful spectacle,
Not even one was killed,
Nobody's blood was spilled.

They related the facts
With blankets on their backs
Shivering from the shame
Of an escape so lame.

The plane they had chartered
Was never recovered;
A blue single engine
From the town of Celgin.

They started a manhunt,
This escape was too blunt
And lots of us took part
But we went losing heart.

After the long efforts
Of the famous cohorts
The long chase came undone
And inmates there were none.

To this very same day,
Two years today this May,
That plane full of inmates
We still ponder its fate.

Lost Love

But I'll go miles, way down the years
Longing for you, hiding my tears,
Chewing upon the happy days,
Just sentence my bleeding heart pays.

Never you'll know; life's so unkind,
How much you remain on my mind.
But in the mean, non-ending while,
I miss your loving, childish smile.

But if ever – God is so good –
You drop by in my neighborhood
And if again from up above
Love swoops down on you like a dove

Then I'll go miles, way down the years
Upon my face showing my cheers,
Inventing lots of lovely ways
To keep you in my arms always.

Unfinished...

So we walked down the road silently, hand in hand,
Nothing was fit to say, so we walked till the end.
Lovely was the sunset upon the autumn trees,
Caressing yet still warm was the afternoon breeze.

The crowd had deserted the narrow, tarless road,
They all had kept their role; off their chests was this load
And they felt with justice, that having been that far
Each one could restfully retreat to his own car.

Peacefully, serenely we walked back to our lives.
We had to piece it back like all good men and wives.
We could declare aloud the torrent in our hearts
But we'd become instead targets for all their darts.

Nothing seems to make sense, nothing, no tear, no cry,
Nothing to give the heart a needed alibi,
Nothing to justify that heartbreaking defeat,
Nothing that would explain the poise in the car seats.

With her she took it all, all the plans, all the dreams,
The laughter, the running, the jumping and the screams.
The eagerness to please when the odds were many,
And her creative skills, stunning and uncanny.

But the death-bearing car of the drunken driver,
Even after hitting and running her over,
Did not stop to assess the crime so cold and vile
But rather dreadfully dragged her for a good mile...

To My Dear Friend

Carry your daily load; bear your parcel of pain
Though it's easy to say, there is no other plan.
Life is a mystery but live it anyway,
Hopefully, joyfully solace will come your way.

I wish I could find words hat would give you courage,
Balm that could heal your wounds, that could appease your rage.
But the simplest of ways it was put to my ears
Is since death's the issue, why go though life in tears?

For you see, this here life, you'll live it anyway.
Choose to laugh, choose to love, all will be well someday.
The hope that He will feed, your courage will sustain
And patience will lead you to the goal to obtain.

You could choose, like many, to retire early,
Take things in your own hands, shorten this tragedy.
But who would perpetrate such a drastic action
Finds out but much too late the eternal sanction.

For condemned they become to never re-enter
Their place of provenance, all their life sought after.
So they drift aimlessly onto oblivion
Having eternally missed their destination.

So carry your burden, help's always on the way,
Never to be denied to those who truly pray
For just like we are here to attest His mercy
The Spirit of our Lord fortifies us daily.

To My Baby

O my lovely,
O my Baby,
You true cause of my lunacy,
You have my nights topsy-turvy,
My days, your name's a litany.

Time after time I see your face
That's when my heart runs a fierce race
Where every beat seems to reveal
The love I carry for you still.

And all the while,
In my exile,
Though between us are many miles,
Your voice of dreams, heavy and mild
Render my thoughts horny and vile.

And from your lips a tender kiss
Recalls to my mind what I miss.
There I remain in lonesome bore
Longing for your warmth and much more.

Say

I long for you, I long for you.
You know how much I long for you?
I long for you that all I do
Is mourn all the times I failed you.

I long for you all my days through
But say, do you do the same too?
My soul always reaching for you
Leaves me weary; I long for you.

Morning Plight

This morning I held you so tight,
I could not, just could not let go.
I did not dream of you last night
But today is one-woman show.

My pillows annoyed by the scene
Did not cradle this déjà vu.
They think you're cold, they think you're mean,
They think…, because they miss you too.

Frankly Speaking

This subject is as old as the human being heart
But unfortunately it sets many apart.
It just that so many making propagandas,
Will not divulge to you their hidden agendas.
So here this diverse crowd made of friends, made of foes
But each and every one with his point of sorrow.
Some claiming "eureka", some with no thoughts at all
But each with conclusions their very own to call.
While we were from day one forewarned on the matter
We fell right in the trap that schised us thereafter.

Frankly speaking, the earth will rotate on its parts
While great minds will come in, and great minds will depart
But to love and forgive and the be tolerant
Should always be our pledge to live well and decent.
Nothing made from this world is ever bound to last
Consequently all things will fade into the past.
So how can we abhor seeing imperfection
When they are at the core of our definition?
From our many flaws is created our mess
But it's all that we have to deal with nonetheless.

Frankly speaking the sound of religion bashing
Should be coming from He who created all things.
Since He 's the only One in whom the Truth resides
To Him but no one else our hearts and wills should glide.

Despair

Just as before
As an encore
I will be ridded of my love.
Just like before
The smile I wore
Is put aside in my alcove.

Never will I act to fathom
In this lifetime of sufferings,
Why some are blest with the boredom
Of tender loving exchanging
Whereas others are depleted
Of every body they treasure
Despite having so long hosted
Of their loving ones the pleasure.
May be the job of my lifetime
Will shed some light on the matter;
Too many times I lost my prime,
Too many times, in my counter.

So here again
With wrenching pain
Of life I've lost the living thrill,
Dreading to meet
A future sweet
Who will take off after her fill.

The Gift

Just a little token
To show you that I care
Just a little token
So you can be aware
That in this life we live,
Just like dear ones depart,
Others come to relieve
Our painful broken hearts.
Hoping this small token
That I finally dare
Bring you love till we can
A deeper friendship share.

Loud And Clear

Loud and clear and all through the years
Solemn vows kindly are exchanged
Loud and clear, struggles, fights and tears
Make married couples so estranged.

Did I Miss You

When I think of the time I did not spend with you,
When I think of the day I left for colder shores
I begin to fathom the logic déjà vu
That absence makes the heart fonder forever more.

The attractions galore, the people are friendly,
The change of the seasons warms even the coldest
With its magical shades transporting merrily
Nature's lovely assets; creation at its best.

But like every season brings its unique sample
Bewildered eyes to see and delectate anew,
Every time you and I meet we receive ample
Of love rendered stronger by kisses overdue.

There famished for a touch, a hug, a tender glance
We feast on each other down to the smallest part.
Nothing can stop the feel or tempo of the dance
When the body and soul melt with its counterpart.

Missing you is therefore the much more needed salt,
The sought after flavor feeding our embrace
And every time my plane connect with the asphalt
I jitter all inside to kiss your lovely face.

Life Without You

Life without you is feasible,
Life without you is possible.
I live because I can wake up
I eat, I sleep and go to work,
Because I play, go to the gym
By my thorough check up it seems
That all is well, that I'm alive.

I live so far because I breathe,
Filling the air with my poor waste
While the rest of the world in haste
Misses that I'm all dead inside
Because you are not by my side.

Life without you is feasible
But I still remain disable.
True that I'm a registered voter,
True that I have a bank account,
True that I have a brand new name
To the others I'm just the same.
I greet people, smiling at times
Barely hiding what goes inside;
Stifling because I'm without you.

Life without you though feasible,
Life without you is horrible.
I go mingle with the others,
I give advice on tough matters,
I help around but all the while
I die daily behind a smile
Surviving carrying the plight
Of somber days and lonely nights
Making up my lifeless living
That I die living without you.

Crosses And Clay

Crosses are sown throughout the Earth
On any given day.
They land and take roots on the turf
Of different shades of clay.
The Potter's love may rearrange
Their depths of anchorage
But always chooses in exchange
To give faith and courage.
For as long as we choose to live
On this traveling sphere
Crosses galore we will receive
Cause of our many tears.

I'll Walk Away

I'll walk away with hurried steps,
I'll walk away, ridded of pep.
I'll walk away; I'll walk away,
I'll walk away one summer's day.
For a long while between us two
There's been no more me and you
And spending time under one roof
Feels like pulling a healthy tooth.

I'll walk away with my lonesome,
With no love, hugging my freedom.
I'll walk away, sniffing the air
All stripped down from this love affair
That keeps me incarcerated.
I'll walk away empty handed
But free from all the glittering;
Money and friends among all things.

I'll walk away without a trace.
For now that love is out of place,
All trampled down, crushed and wasted,
The spirit's left all deflated.
But since at every sun that shines
We receive all; what's yours, what's mines,
One summer's day though lacking pep
I'll walk away with hurried steps.

One Of These Days

One of these days before your eyes,
One of these days of sudden light,
One of these days you'll realize
The true meaning of this here plight.
Do not fall apart if at all
The same one who you so despise
Is the one who answers the call
Of lonely soul deprived of ties.

Often they say that who you meet
On the way up of any road,
On the way down another street
Often helps you carry your load.
Life is always what you know best;
A never-ending mystery.
But the care that you give the rest
Comes back in form of His mercy.

So live your life, be your own boss,
Do what you must, follow your will
But always keep in mind the cross
When so often you lose your thrill.
One of these days before your eyes,
One of these days feeling His might,
One of these days you'll get your prize
But for now, please, bear this here plight.

Loving You

I'll love you forever no matter where you are,
I'll love you forever, be you near, be you far.
I'll love you forever, this is what I live for
I'll love you when you'll be nothing but just a core.

My heart has forever beaten to your cadence,
It remains ectopic without your radiance.
I'll love you forever till you live our midst
I'll love you still after you will cease to exist.

Say It

Say it with words, say it aright,
Say it and watch her smile spring bright.
Say it well the very first time,
Say it using the perfect rhyme.

Father

*For all the highs and lows
Of this life here below
Sure You never forsake
From giving them a break.*

*Steadily Your kindness
Counteracts their dryness,
You've been the good Father
Whose Love never falters.*

*You sustain, You provide
Despite their human pride
Breaking the harmony
Since they won't bend the knee.*

Your Spell

I should attempt to tell
The grasp you have on me.
How kept under your spell
My heart too jittery
Keeps me deprived of rest.

When you decide to come
And nudge my starving soul
I can never fathom
My loss of self-control,
The chaos within my chest.

I can never foresee
When or where you'll decide
To come back and fetch me
When from your hold I glide
And evade from your nest.

For every time you call
My whole world becomes still
And on my knees I fall
To receive my love fill
From the one I love best

Come

Come, come, come to me
And I will tell you
Every ounce of pain
The soul can obtain
When he finds himself
Without the soul mate
That he so adores

Come, oh come and see
And I will show you
The hellish desert
That he had to cross
Knowing that he lost
The only creature
Born to his measure.

Come, come already
And appraise the trance
That only your eyes,
His most precious prize,
Can instill in him…
That's the silent scream
Of his love for you.

To You Again

To this love given to my life,
This precious chosen companion,
Silent escort on this long path
Leading me right back to Zion,

To the God sent little angel,
Bearing His love upon her wings,
Willing so kindly to travel
The length of miles thus remaining,

To the joyful dove hovering
Over the dullness of my soul,
Promising so many treasure
And so willing to pay my toll

To this rare pearl finally found
To finalize my diadem
Who brought me of Heaven the sound
Within her voice that always tames

Whatever drives deep within me,
I give my heart, mind and body
And though the world may disagree
I give my soul complete and free.

Sudden Voyage

Saddled up by your love,
Blindfolded by my heart
I came at the sounds of
Your sighs stinging like darts.

I had to rush to see,
Had to prove to my world
That though felt silently
You were my true dream girl.

So I came and just poured
My heart hidden treasures
Before you I adore,
You, made at my measure.

I promise then to love
To cherish and honor
You, precious little dove,
You, queen of my manor

For saddled by your love
I need but one rider
Who with her gentle gloves
Will make my heart fonder.

Love's Coin

For it's only when the heart bleeds
That you're aware that you're in love.
It's only when love plants its seeds
That your soul fits hers like a glove.

So you stifle when you're alone
For you miss the air that she breathes.
Since your will to live is all gone
Your emotions are put to freeze.

For you're shivering all inside
Lacking the warmth of her presence
And swallowing your foolish pride
You call and call with insistence.

And you go on to perpetrate
The smallest of her daily acts.
This feeds the never-ending state
Of good times you want to bring back.

But don't despair, oh don't be sad,
Rejoice instead and pray it lasts,
This case is far from being bad;
It's healthy for the heart to fast.

Only then you become aware
Of the depths of the love you share.
I know, my friend, it is not fair
But love stings when you truly care.

So go, nurture your achy heart,
Yearn day and night, and night and day,
Yearn for the hand of your sweetheart
Deep in your heart she'll always stay.

And as often, before you know,
Before your feelings consume you
Around you she'll joyfully throw
Her embrace fed by love so true.

For only when the soul withers
You are aware of where you stand.
Rejoice then that your heart suffers
The two extremes that love commands.

Mahogany Queen

I wish so much, so much my dear
To have you close and hold you near
And right into your brown eyes peer
And encounter your naked soul.

So long, so long I hungered for,
For you to come dock to my shore,
A simple gesture from a door
Ajar, straight from my many strolls.

But each and every time I'd round
Mainly to see where you'd be found,
You'd simply evade this poor hound
Who'd go back then to his abode.

And silently there, in my den,
I'd pray so hard, I'd pray often
That you'd show up in some sudden
So you could see my yearning load.

But in this jungle, this sheer maze
Of heeding bells and serving trays
I'd peep onto your floor in daze
Of my sole mahogany queen.

Then satiated for just sometime
I'd go back just before the chime
Of the cell phone reveal where I'm
And hope again for the same scene.

My Oath

I'll love you silently,
I'll love you on the side.
I'll love you and you'll see
Of my love the strong tide.

There is only one you,
The others away fade.
The only thing to do
Is to stay in your shade.

I'll love you, my jolie,
Of this you should be proud.
Thanks for having swiftly
Pulled my soul from this shroud.

When She Calls

And suddenly she calls
And my restlessness falls
So fast that my speech stalls;
She's all I want to hear.
Blest is the one lonely
When he receives daily
What he treasures dearly;
"Hello" from the one dear.

It comes just like the dew
And quenches within you
The yearning for the Boo
That's so hard to carry.
It comes to ease the pain
When the heart and soul strain
From lacking the refrain
Of her voice so merry.

So little does she know
That the simple echo
Of her lovely solo
Can change the man in you,
The pet that you've become
Always hungers for some
Of her chew. The fewsome
Then wag a tail or two.

If ever she would fail
To send her lovely "hail",
The mayhem that'd entail
At times can be deadly.
For there have been cases
In not so far places
Of death leaving traces
Of heart stifled slowly.

That is why when she calls,
Before the timbre falls
I get right on the ball
And answer to my Boo
For if dying is tough
Nothing can be more rough
Than the questions she'd cough
Drilling you through and through.

Surrender

Lord of my soul to You I surrender.
Deep in Your love Lord I find my pleasure.
Come and take control, I'll live a better
Vision of what You see for me.

Into my heart Lord let Your dwelling be
So that the world can see Your stamp on me.
From my bondage O Lord, please set me free
So I can serve you faithfully.

Your Word my Lord is anchored in my mind.
Under Your tent my solace I will find
I have struggled to leave the world behind
And follow closely where You trod.

But in the midst of chaos and worries
Often O Lord I drift and I'm sorry.
Help me always to come in a hurry
Back into Your blessed accord.

In the shade of Your bottomless mercy
I'll grow closer to You, Savior daily,
Striving to be the best version of me,
For the journey valuable load.

And finally when I am safely home,
I'll sing Your praises, to You, the Awesome,
At last among Your selected fewsome
When forever will be the mode.

Flight From The City

When there is nothing left
But an attempted theft
That sadly had gone left
Then it's time for goodbye.
It's easy to notice.
They could have hidden this
From the blindest novice;
It was clear to the eye.

But though it's hard to take
And you can feel the ache
You have yourself to shake
From out this dreaded spot.
When the signs are so clear
You have to frankly veer
For peace of mind so dear
Whether you're brave or not.

And when you're far away
Please remember to stay
Silent as a sought prey,
Far away from that den.
There ponder silently
The blessed way you flee
A danger so deadly
That your heart could've smitten

And from now keep in mind
To run and leave behind
Any similar bind
Cause of insanity.
Better safe than sorry
This way you won't hurry
To jot down such story;
Your flight from the City.

Been a While

Been a while since I heard from you,
Been a while but then tell me who
Could predict the start or the end
Of an idyll hard to pretend.

As often in this world of fools,
Sadly it's only one who drools
And the other, just being kind,
Toys subtly with his or her mind.

And the game goes on for a while
Depending on the players' style.
No one gets hurt, no one gets caught
And at the end there is no tight knot.

But more than often I can say
It's more sad than the come what may.
More than often we don't pretend,
More than often, we're in deep end

Begging desperately to be saved
Either from deep sea or the grave
When who's waving at the rivage
Strikes a low blow to your old age.

So we'll go on our separate way
Or so it seems, to my dismay.
Either way I have to explain
How dear to me that you remain.

I've never been stricken so hard,
I've never stood there, such retard,
Not knowing what to say or do
Just like the first day I saw you.

Our Eyes

*Never will I dare to forget
The warm evening I first saw you.
Deep in my mind I dearly pet
This memory kept strong and new.*

*Everything led to this meeting,
The universe was well aligned.
Every living soul stopped breathing,
That time just for us was designed.*

*So when I set my eyes on you,
Loveliest creature on two feet,
A clean slate was handed brand new
Right when the first time our eyes meet.*

The Spark

When He first set the spark
Deep and strong in my heart,
I was branded the mark
Of your love from the start.

I know I was begging
For the love of my live
But such a true feeling
Of you, breath can deprive.

It came daring and loud,
As brutal as lightning,
Stood tall above the crowd
Of all previous feelings.

Love of alike nature
Engulfs you at first sight.
They strike with no measure,
They hit with all their might.

So when I got the spark
That burst deep in my heart,
Sure even in the dark
I saw a brand new start.

The Bliss

When they accost my mind,
The jolly thoughts of you,
My spirit that they find
Is always made brand new.

They quickly redirect
My whole life to one sight,
The tableau so perfect
Of your face, their delight.

There they always linger,
Leaving me in a daze
Where they feed my hunger
And set my heart ablaze.

So when deep in my mind
Thoughts of you take a dive,
Right in this bliss I find
I thank God I'm alive.

I Could

I could bombard you with my thoughts,
Reveal the many times I sought
Of your hand and mine tie the knot,
Live happily after.

I could dismantle all the norms,
The ones society transforms,
In jail so humans can perform
Like birds of one feather.

I could tear down every barrier
And get our hearts so merrier,
Leaving a life so much freer,
You for me, me for you.

I could pulverize the concept,
The ones that got you to accept
Subtly society precepts
Upheld your whole life through.

Only I rather, my sweet dove,
Just pray daily that your sweet love
Be sent to me right from above
Bind us one another.

The Bug

I'd tell you of this bug I caught
But I'm afraid you'd rather not
From your daily chores be distraught
So I'll remain silent.
I'd tell you but then first of all
You have to promise not to fall
Among those who of laughter, bawl
With no solid intent.

See twas a day like one of those
And spring was coming to a close
So with no real motive I chose
To do what I do best.
I showed up at the job on time,
Chattered a bit for thus I am,
Gathered everything then, all primed,
I left the nursing nest.

Like every day I chose to stop
First of all at the very top,
This strategy I had adop'
Ted from the very start
So two floors below on my round
That's when I was knocked to the ground,
I knew it when I felt the pound'
Ing in my very heart

Twas not the kind you get rid of,
Neither was it the ones you shove
But deep inside, the mazel tov
Was rather out of place.
So on my round I continued,
Weak at the knees and yet renewed
Of having contacted the new
Sweet bug all of us chase.

Speak To Me Softly

Speak softly to me
Speak to me gently
Tell me about you
Your old and your new
New that brought us two
And made you my Boo
Speak of your worries
The deep winter freeze
Speak of your secret
Things I don't know yet
Things we may never
Tell one another
Things that make me blush
And my ego crush

Speak of your sadness
That comes to harness
Your heart I long for
Stronger than before
Like a shooting star
In the heavens far
Miracle of light

In your eyes so bright
Glance that swiftly glide
That we try to hide
Revealing anew
My hunger of you
That tends to translate
The short of our fate.

Speak of you freely
One day my lovely
Letting me explore
Like never before
Your peachy garden
I dreamt of often.
Savor your essence
With long impatience
Glide over the stars
Still in heavens far
First hand experience
Rhythmic wining dance
That's bound to explode
In heaven's abode.

At Stranger

You had me at "stranger"
That was all I hoped for
A sign short and meager
That would set the fervor
I had kept deep inside.

You had me at "stranger"
And I was suddenly
Lost at sea no longer.
Had eyes for you only,
Something I could not hide.

You had me at "stranger"
But ignored the effect
Your voice blessed candor
And melodious affect
Of my heart became guide.

Like a wooden puppet,
Remotely well fingered
I was th'elated pet
Whose mistress had lingered,
Jumping from side to side

But let the whole world know,
With no fuss, no ringer,
That my heart took the blow
When I heard your "stranger",
This I claim with great pride.

Of This World

For the best of the world,
The world will be their best
But the rest of the world
The world will not give rest.

Their treasure and their hearts
Will be wrapped in this world
For their hearts find treasure
In things the world offers
And the things they treasure
Will be heart of their world.

Darkest Hour

Ah! So sweet the nothings, so true the endearments
Uttered by my Junie, chasing all my torments!
Spirits of the nineties, who tested our romance,
Have you pleaded with God to give us one more chance?

The years were so young yet, but the wills were so strong.
New york shined in the fall, but Doylestown still belong'
To the fervent Christians at every first Friday.
Clearwater yet remained far, far away at bay.

The plans were so steady and the hearts so willing.
All seemed to be arranged, none that'd still need nailing.
The horizon afar seemed day by day closer;
No doubts were on the minds, the world knew I chose her.

Before the Lord of love we planned to seal it all.
Twas all said, twas all done from what I still recall.
But in a cruel sudden came the unthinkable;
The cold blade in the back, our plans to disable.

And all came tumbling down, and ever since remained
All tarnished, damp and cold, with soul forever stained.
But He who sees the heart in its true contrition,
In mercy will restore all to His volition.

Therefore the faith remains, as blind as faith can be.
Strong enough to sustain, strong enough to foresee
The ingenious plan of the good Lord of Hosts
From whom nothing escapes, even tricks of cheap ghosts.

With A Gift

With all the love for a lady
Comes this token on Christmas Eve
Just to reveal to my baby
My heart resting upon my sleeve.

So please, receive this little charm,
Petty proof of my love for you.
Let it gently your spirit warm
And remain with you all life through.

My Lovely Little Bird

O my baby Erie
My sweet little chérie
You came breathe life in me
You taught my heart to sing the loveliest of symphony,
You took it for a spin with your angelic voice,
You kissed my breath away to forever-spring land.
The melodious sound
Of the tone of your words
Reminds me that I found
A pearl from all these herds.
The glow of your brown eyes
Reveals now free of lies
That heaven does exist.
I can never resist
The softness of your hands
But no one understands
Why it's you
Again you
Always you
You, you, you.

I live in slow motion each time
Of your voice I don't hear the chime.
My world remains a mere shadow
Till you step in it tomorrow.
Then just as suddenly
My joy comes back again
Cause baby you have me
In the palm of your hand.

None Else More

Open your ears, lovely maiden, open your ears,
Open your ears so his serenade you can hear,
Open your ears; this is your beggar standing here;
Him alone, none else more.

Open your ears, my lady fair, open your ears
He comes daring, from her sweet dream, his angel steer,
He comes ado declaring his love to you, dear,
You alone, none else more.

Open your eyes, my angel fine, open your eyes,
Open your eyes and see in him there's no disguise.
Open your eyes and of his heart come see the size
Beat for you, none else more.

Open your eyes, my tweedy bird, open your eyes,
Open your eyes; he comes out loud so please arise.
Open your eyes for here alone he feels chastised
By you and none else more.

Open your door, O my sunshine, open your door,
Open your door and like you've never done before
Receive the love that on this night he comes to pour
At your feet, none else more.

Open your door, my sweetie pie, open your door,
Open your door; hear his voice to the heavens soar.
This night is cold but thoughts of you, whom he adores,
Comfort him, none else more

*Heaven and Earth, lovely Pumpkin, Heaven and Earth
Are here tonight, of this love, to bless the rebirth.
Open your heart, for much too long he missed your mirth,
Cuddle and so much more.*

"What Is This?"

From the many blows I received
To all the lovers I deceived,
The love that for you my heart bears
Favors pure celestial affairs.

Who would have thought that in a glance
We'd be caught in this jolly dance?
When in the rapture of this bliss
I humbly wonder: "What is this?"
My soul amidst all this frenzy
Reminds my tipsy heart softly:

"Love is the quintessential gift
That mercifully is bequeathed
To the one who though suffering
From the Lord still expect all things.

"Therefore don't think your heart's at stakes
When lovingly your hand she takes;
You just received from God above
His blessed and once-promised love."

Sweeter Than You

Sweeter than you, kinder than you,
I traveled far, as far can be,
Searching, searching for someone who
Would dare swim the troubled sea
Your candid heart dared to sail through.

Sweeter than you, but tell me who
In this lifetime has ever thought
That in your stead, unique, brand new,
Nobody else so far has brought
This love as sweet as honeydew.

Sweeter than you, all this life through,
With words and knees bent at your feet,
Though far away I search ado,
Faithfully I'll wait for my treat
And live this love that I once knew.

Sing Alleluia

Give thanks; give thanks to our Lord,
He gives us what we can't afford.
His love for us knows no boundary,
He longs to show us His mercy.

So many times we hear His call
But many times we fail and fall
But He, the merciful Father
Forgets His creatures but never.

He gives us His mighty Spirit
Which our poor nature completes.
Throughout our lives He sustains us
That in His eyes we remain just.

He repeatedly when we pray
Strengthens us in our dismay
And lovingly stands us steady
Amidst our own sin misery.

So many times He gives us sight
Of His great Love, Power and Might
But senselessly we come up short
Of His truth we often contort.

So sing praises to our God,
Give thanks to the Almighty Lord.
Towards us He shows his kindness
And gives us lots of His richness.

Then make a testimony leap
For if a king's treasure's to keep
The work of God we should declare,
With the whole world His graces share.

Hurry

Hurry and give your life to me,
Hurry my dear, time is at hand.
Hurry before spring leaves the land
And slides into dichotomy.

Hurry and give your life to me,
Come give me my fulfilling dose
For if the petals yield the rose
Surely our days will be balmy.

Hurry and give your life to me
For if ever angels are sent
To straighten what's been so far bent,
They'd have your lovely eyes Mammy.

Hurry and give your life to me
Then in the stillness of the nights
We'll set our world of stars aright,
Right on the lake of Dulcamy.

To You

I stand before you, knocking at your door,
I stand before you as I did before.
I stand before you, all naked and poor
With only my love sung as an encore.

Repeatedly I hear: "Go your own way,
I'm living my life, find yours in the hay.
You left it down there, acting so foolish,
Be a man for once, it's over, finished."

But here I still stand like a lonely dog
All afraid to go and face the thick fog.
I have one mistress, a lovely lady,
How can I ever exist or be me
If she doesn't hold secure of my leash;
I'd surely one day, get lost and perish.

O darling I beg, listen to my plea,
It's again the voice of your poor baby
Coming back to life from his misery
And praying out loud for you to marry.

You know if ever I had another,
Never but never would they make waver
This heart beating strong but for you only
Which if in your hands would be so merry.
Honey I just can't forget about you.
God knows how I tried, tried to start anew
But always your face, so sweet in my hands,

Eclipse all others who between us stand.
I will forever beg for your pardon
And don't ask me why and for what reason
You should to my plea give your attention.
I'd gladly reply – no hesitation –
Listen to your heart for there still resides
The love of me you so hard tried to hide.

I often picture this blessed evening
When my eyes on you will do a landing.
The stars in the sky will surely rejoice
And in their own way will second your choice.

This world will remain a sorrowful place,
It will rain sometimes, the moon won't change face.
The sun will always warm us with its rays
But even among this known disarray
I know with your love, the world will be kind
For the sole reason that you're on my mind.

If only you knew how much I cherish
The fall when it puts on leaves its finish.
This just reminds me of you my baby,
See how much I learnt from you, my Junie.

I'll try not to bore you any longer
Though I spilled my guts unlike no other
I hope that within your heart you still have
The strength you once had to show me the path
Back into your arms. For there I desire
Comes rain or comes shine to live the entire
Rest of this ordeal that you call my life
Hoping that safe there, I'll settle my strife.

I stand before you, knocking at your door,
I stand before you like never before.
I stand before you with my heart still sore.
I stand before you hear my poor downpour.

Rhyming

Though it so much tickles the ears
Rhyming just does not make a poem.
But if away from it you steer
Your wave will crash then with no foam.

Thus rhyming is to the reader
The icing on a tasty cake.
The whole desert is much sweeter,
Enhancing the dough you just bake'.

The choice of rhyme does not matter
As much as how it does surprise
The reader who comes takes shelter
Within the lines they render wise.

Often it shows the skillfulness
Of the writer's inspiration;
Showing that they have more or less
Used wit and imagination.

It is given high importance
In certain school of great poetry
But in some much modern romance
The stress is placed on the sultry.

But as it in the classic case,
One swims in the sea of one's choice.
The clever bird will show its face
Only to a familiar voice.

One never pulls out of his hat
The rabbit they never possess'
But if they pulled many – so what,
Let your ears enjoy the caress.

Their Plight

Now that it came to your backyard
As it did for so many times,
Now that it made you feel awkward
You ask me to jot a few rhymes

On the riveting videos
Passed around all over the Net.
They smacked your Haitian ego
And your human heart, they upset.

But if they offend the public
It's just that the cellphone era
Renders any news too epic
Hence the dark cloud on your aura.

But I assure you my dear friend,
Though upsetting, tis no big deal.
The world down to its very end
Will stage such atrocities still.

The human being has deep inside
This well rooted dark tendency
To crush the weak ones at his side
Once he is in majority.

See the plight of the Israelites
Pulled from the snares of the Pharaoh
And that of the Africanites
From the slaves and now the ghettos.

Remember well the genocides
For reasons that reason ignores,
Done repeatedly, done with pride,
Done for reasons the world abhors.

The other one always delights
Each and every time he succeeds
At cashing on the human plight,
Use it, his darkest self to feed.

Yes it's shocking and appalling
To see the dark one in action
But what kills you seeing these scenes
Is not the mere situation

But rather the fact that you saw
What otherwise you'd only hear.
It leaves a long sounding echo
That away from you just won't steer.

But the Earth and its nastiness
Will stay on its trajectory
As long as humans are possess'
They'll feed their beast in a hurry.

The Love Of God

The love of God in us remain
Despite loads of sorrow and pain.
Day after day He sustains us,
Keeps us humble if not pious.

The love of God is here to stay
And daily invites us to pray.
For only praying fortifies
The soul in us, which always sighs.

The love of God is a free gift
Giving us a much needed lift,
Helping us carry the burden
Done to us by all the brethren.

The love of God will see us through
For in this life we have no clue
Of what's ahead. But He uttered
To follow Him to the Father.

The love of God then I'll cherish.
The love of God will establish
Upon the Earth bless´ed wisdom
Of Peace and Love, His true Kingdom.

Sheer Clemency

And so it goes, and so it goes
That in this world of foes
Always surges a friend,
A God sent of kindness and love
Who gently will come shove
And take you to the end.

And so it goes, and so it goes
That the Almighty shows
His mercy to His kids
And when you think that all is done
And every hope is gone
He shows His mighty deeds.

And so it goes, and so it goes,
I will follow you close,
My lovely guiding light
For when you set your eyes on me,
Through blesséd alchemy,
Ran out all my fright.

And so it goes, God only knows.
The blessings He bestows
Come down from His mercy.
Just when I though my life had passed
Just like a loving blast
Came down His clemency.

My Treat

After eating have something sweet;
That's her routine of every day.
As though to reward with a treat
Her lovely taste buds in dismay.

After eating then, on her feet,
Casually she just threw my way
Whatever she feels I merit
Solely to chase my blues away.

So eat on but have something sweet
But I'm hoping she comes my way;
For she remains the only treat
I want to have day after day.

Nothing

Nothing can come close to the thrill,
Nothing, when from your mind you drill.
Nothing when finally you feel
The outcome of your creation.

Nothing, when words you don't possess
With pen to paper gives caress
And to your eyes, in turn impress,
When you face the inspiration.

Nothing compares to the time spent,
Nothing, when there, under your tent
You savor the idea content
When mind and muse make connection.

Nothing I say, nothing on earth
Is more thrilling than to give birth
To the thoughts hidden in her girth;
Essence of her revelation.

From nothing then to blesséd some,
My dear I promise I will come
Always to offer your bosom
The bouquet of my emotions.

Your Face

I often consider from the depths of my heart
The reasons why I melt, losing all assurance,
Find it hard to focus, like having an infarct,
Fighting for every word, almost like in a trance.

Yet this inner snafu, this internal chaos
Causing my heart to gear, racing the Daytona,
Provokes in my psyche a strong surge of pathos,
Leaving me weak, faintly, just like a madonna.

This mother of feeling of my throat grabs a hold
And the knot I swallow seems to have many peers
And the smile I expose seems to favor pure gold
For it comes underline my many inner fears.

And I feel I could kneel; I'd be so much closer
To the ground that I feel I might hit anytime.
Since it is the posture adequate for prayer,
I pray hoping my voice rings not like a fake chime.

Painfully I attempt to show some composure.
I had always excelled at keeping it inside
And slowly deliver, carefully, with measure,
This gush of affection, the love I cannot hide.

But deep within my eyes I know it can be seen,
The lovely, jolly cause of my discountenance.
Come and look into them and enjoy the whole scene;
Your pretty face my dear, of divine countenance.

Tobago, Damn!

And if I write this poem deprived of any bliss
It's just to celebrate you, the one that I miss.
If I compose this poem with love as a main theme,
You'll come into my arms, right out of my dream.

I often reminisce that time when we were two,
When everything we did was so thrilling to you.
You were always present at every occasion,
Ignoring so often the sense of time notion.
But I should know I'd miss you so
When you took off to Tobago.

If I pour my heart today, facing this crowd,
It's for them to tell you how I miss you out loud.
If every word I say is sprinkled with sadness
I hope they make you run right back into your nest.

I remember so well the long walks on the beach,
You and I, hand in hand, good time I still cherish.
You barefoot in the sand, your hand clenching your skirt,
Jumping at every wave, frowning at every dirt
That in the sea they often throw
Up here, just like in Tobago.

If I write down these lines as a desperate plea,
It's for you to return, bring your love back to me.
If I write that I fade without your love my dear,
It's for you to hurry come bring life over here

Where my world makes no sense, time is at a stand still,
The sun has lost its shine and fall has no appeal.
No shower in April to light your month of May,
The beach so full of dirt, the steel drums gone away.
Life strives under blankets of snow
While it's blooming in Tobago.

Nighterie

The music is in my head
Do you dig it,
Beating up with pacing stead;
All ears get it.

The flowery maze here below
Confused the potential foes.
They came while they stayed aboard,
Will not walk where they once trod
Crowd of gentle folks in awe
Releasing frustration in "Oh's".

The music stopped in my head
In a sudden
Right there lying in my bed
I grasp its trend.

But in the maze here below
One can still hears the ramble
Of the crowd ceasing to roar
The sadness that we see soar…
In the midst of this nighterie
The alarm rings with fury.

One Day

One of these days will spring, one of these blesséd days,
One special day made of pure laughter on the rocks.
Of day of mid-autumn, of untangled dreadlocks,
One day of sheer blossom, of essence of Olay.

One day that stands alone and carries its burden,
One day of pure thin air and low humidity.
One day with saddle fine and solid unity,
One day of gardenias over a toddle's den.

One blesséd blue-sky day with bed of scented rose,
One day of Christmas Eve with magi in limo.
One precious day of days with more highs than of lows,
One day inspiring all the rhymes and the prose.

One day that would render other days pitiful,
One day that'd make amend for futuristic faults.
One day just like the day that'd open heaven's vault
And put you in my arms, free, loving and peaceful.

Listen…

*I could tell you one day
How empty and senseless
Life can be without you.
I could tell you to stay
For my world becomes less
Dreary, my sky turns blue…
But to tell you all this
Would you ever believe,
Take it in or dismiss?*

*I could show you one day
How quickly I regress
To nothing until you
With your angelic way
And your kisses that bless
Come and give me brand new
Hope and strength that I miss
Cause from you I receive
My sorrow and my bliss.*

*Many more than one way
Lead to sheer happiness
But they hurt through and through.
This love that you display
With genuine gentleness
Springs life in me anew
So thank God for all this,
This treasure I retrieve,
Like a sacred chalice.*

The Right Time

The right time never fails,
The right time never trails.
It's always so punctual
To display the usual
Load of kronos power
To tackle whatever
Befalls a certain one
Whose task is still undone.

The right time never tries
To provoke the demise
Of the time it follows.
It is always too close
To the time that is born
Right after. But it scorns
The futuristic plans
That are built up in vain.

The right time will always
Question the dragging ways
We delay the action
Under its dominion.
So it kindly reminds
The aftermath that hinds
Frank procrastination
And besets deception.

The right time will provoke
With repeated strokes
The waking of the will
Power of genuine steel.
For only a solid,
Determined, intrepid
Can profit of its span
And concretize the gain.

The right time won't perish.
It conveys what's cherished
To the moment in line,
With a similar spine
Well able to carry
The task that's in query.
It tries to dissipate
The scent of being late.

The right time will prevail
And set us on the trail
Of desired success,
Displaying our prowess.
The right time of our love
Will come straight from above
To kiss the bleeding hearts
That it once set apart.

Generescence

Lift high the mental image,
Kept in your heart storage.
Lift high the cherished notion
That set the turn of seasons.

Keep safe the factual contrast
That makes motivation last;
They simbiose each other
But always beg to differ.

Then at every occasion
You experience the notion
Of a different atmosphere
Clashing with the one that's here.

It's as strong as night and day,
As black and white always stays.
This concept of head and tail
Keeps us humans on the trail.

It prevents curséd boredom,
Gives us drive till Kingdom come,
Veers into the wrong and right
And sets good and evil bright.

So thank God for this notion
That helps to move creation.
It promotes generescence
And of life is the essence.

Your Eyes

Every blessing the Lord bestows
Declares out loud His love for us,
Through the joys and through the sorrows
With His spirit deep within us.

More then often in His wisdom
He goes surpassing His mercies
And so the blesséd outcome
Lingering unbelief, defreeze'

Nothing on Earth says it louder,
Nothing His blesséd love can size,
Nothing can attest it better
Than the look I see in your eyes.

God's Love

Funny how it feels so strong
What we thought did not belong
Tween the both of us.

You remain the pinnacle
I thought could never tackle
If I'd die and burst.

But the love planted in us
Is an all miraculous
Gift from God above.

He created you and me
So that through monogamy
We may feel His love.

Intuition

Sometimes we try to write a thought
But bright ideas we gather naught
Though high and low some help we sought
That'd suffocate our blankness.
But sad enough we realize
How writing can be mythicized
Robbing us of our precious prize
Underlining the mind staleness.

For pen alone cannot draw near
The vivid scenes that the mind steers,
The dreadfulness of inner fears,
The ones our daily lives reflect.
We make usage of masks galore,
Pretend, cover but in our core,
Well-hidden like strong metaphors,
Scrutiny we barely deflect.

For intuition never cease'
To capture what we don't release,
Spirits to spirits always tease
In so doing nature's exchange
And so we go our laden way
Carrying around what we don't say,
Feigning to the world come what may
But to the same nothing is strange.

The story of our provenance
Will clarify at a mere glance
The nature of this occurrence
That has baffled generations.
For time and again is revealed
This solemn truth that should have healed
The world for we carry concealed
Our true identification.

Nursing

Never has it been seen
Until Flo intervene'
Revealing profession
Without compensation.
Invest for tomorrow,
Nurture the weak in health;
God will give you His wealth.

Sometimes

Sometimes I feel so far apart,
Disconnected,
Searching earnestly in my heart
Though dejected
Not finding someone to connect
But in my soul
I still feel the divine effect
That makes me whole.

So when alone I reach inside
And grab a hold
Of the Light who in me abides
As I've been told.
And all in a blesséd sudden
My loneliness
Merges into a peaceful den
Of happiness.

Mirage

*Conversing on the phone, fell in love with the voice,
Hoping it'd be surging from an adequate source.
I could not help myself, did not have any choice
Admiring this face, my heart increased in force.*

*Ravishing, beautiful, exquisitely jovial,
Over the ones I've known you reign as prettiest.
Sincerely I love you; please won't you be my pal?
Silently I will wait; my poor heart will not rest.*

When They're Gone

The emptiness they live behind,
The vacuum when you cannot find
The loved one for whom you so pine
Is to the mind so disturbing.

The emptiness you fall into
Whenever that dear you know who
Decides to see no more of you,
Cause of your visceral tearing

You physically feel you're drowning,
Desperately you are air gasping,
Trying to hold to anything
Your shattered world, reconciling.

But nothing can come and replace
The voice nor the familiar face
Whose souvenirs you can't erase
And get back to daily living…

The emptiness they left behind
Will so disturb my lonely mind
And put my poor heart in a bind
Of against these odds, keep beating.

Don't Shed Tears

Don't shed the tears, my heart,
Come out of your alcove.
Don't shed the tears, my heart
Don't be afraid to love;
Her heart may be fickle,
Drift away a little,
Let it go, let it go!

Don't shed the tears, my heart,
Regain your composure.
Don't she the tears, my heart,
Beat at the same measure;
Time always comes to heal
The worst pain you might feel
And frees us from sorrow.

Don't shed the tears, my heart,
Come, come and dry your tears.
Don't shed the tears, my heart,
Bring to the Lord your fears.
In many ways before
For love of you He bore
Your burdens long ago.

A Lovely Day

A lovely day is of all time
Remarkable at every hour.
From the first time of alarm chime
You take a feel of its power.

Every fiber of your being
Receives the message loud and clear.
Soundlessly it comes declaring:
"Hey, I am here so have no fear."

It bounces off at each moment
Trying to relate the message
Of the Love of whom it was sent
To touch every other visage.

The odds that might steps in its way
They just magically disappear.
All the pros towards it just sway;
They know a lovely day is here.

So my child, have a lovely day,
Of anything may you not brood.
Take gratefully what's yours today
From the Father of all that's good.

My Abducted Child

On that day you were born
I was busy working,
Jill you were the first one;
It was a proud feeling.

The child you then became
Was our pride and joy.
For nothing we could blame
Our sweet little tomboy.

We planned ahead for you,
Did it all from our hearts.
Before our dreams come true
They were shattered in parts.

The last time you were seen
You exited the store.
You wore the cut top green
You had the day before.

Some kids even recall
Having seen you walk by.
You threw them back their ball
And then waved them goodbye.

Some said they saw that car
Driving around slowly.
It then parked not too far
The "sharp knife" butchery.

They could not remember,
Others did not bother.
We just could not explain
What happened to you then.

They said they saw you turn
Right around the green bar.
Others claimed that they yearn'
For what we felt so far.

But none could experience
What I felt deep inside;
That deep visceral trance
That courage could not hide.

And the day passed us by
We all barked at the moon
And we saw the months fly
They were so full of gloom.

Your mother in distress
Wanted to end her life.
She became such a mess,
Lost all her inner drive.

Then came that true solace
From the good Lord we pray,
He sent to us our Grace
On a warm summer's day.

She came three years after
On that same Tuesday eve,
Became the little flower
We thought could not conceive.

She had your lovely eyes,
Your place she'll never fill,
This angel in disguise,
Sent by God, my sweet Jill.

Whenever you may be
This poem's written to you
Will tell you my baby
Of how much we love you

The crosses carried often
Come crashing on our heads.
They're for us to obtain
Merits to keep God's treads.

Deep In Her Soul

Siting alone all day
Reviewing deep inside
The dreary shades of gray
And all that they can hide,

She gives space a long stare,
Unwilling to control
This pressing lack of care
From her dejected soul.

Nothing seems to matter,
Nothing makes any sense.
Nothing can upset her,
For nothing is worth pence.

Blazé her perspective,
Trivial her train of thoughts.
Uttered words just deceive
So she'd rather hear naught.

Then sitting all alone
She attends her bruised mind.
To her life is all done,
She left nothing behind.

Things she so much cherished,
Things she held in esteem.
Things she kept on a leash
Drowning her silent screams.

So it faded away
Whatever life she had.
Gray clouds are here to stay
Making her feel so sad.

O Lord

How lovely are Your ways, O Lord,
Towards those who truly love You!
How lovely, since this love they lord
Is from day one a gift from You!

How lovely are Your ways, O Lord,
And naught can beat this blessèd truth,
That always with divine accord
Daily their every ill You soothe.

You hatch this love deep in their hearts
So they gladly take up their cross.
Of Your plans they don't know the parts
But of their lives they know the Boss.

How lovely are Your ways, O Lord,
Towards those who truly love You!
Lead us to Your divine abode,
Us who have put our trust in You.

Mighty Deeds

And for a long, long time
We waited for this time.
Time of peace, time of joy,
Time free of least alloy,
Time that will make us see
That among the many
Who came seeking a break
We too had what it takes
To make it yet so far
While many lost their star.

For long, long time ago,
Searching high, searching low,
We always came up short
Of peace of any sort.
So we went on faking
To all the human beings
While what we had inside
Was nothing else but pride
And the sole reason why
Peace to us was so shy.

*But now we understand,
It's been so well explained,
That what you so receive
And that so often grieves
Is drawn from the many
Actions that we carry.
So always keep in mind
That you ought to be kind
For our deeds have power
To bring tears or laughter.*

Souvenirs

Should always remember
Your days of love fever
For in life if ever
Your loved one moves farther,
Causing you to wither
You will have thereafter
Souvenirs to treasure

Dear Lord

It's always unannounced
O my beloved Lord,
It's always unannounced
That from divine accord,
It's always unannounced
That Your children You nudge.

For Your divine mercy,
Mercy we don't deserve,
For Your divine mercy,
Heavenly grace reserves,
For your divine mercy
Carries us with no grudge.

Your unending goodness
Roaming over the Earth,
Your unending goodness,
Following us from birth,
Your unending goodness
Is so just when You judge

That Lord under Your wings
Forever we'll remain,
That Lord under Your wings
Is the safest heaven
That Lord under Your wings
All through our life we'll drudge.

Blessed Assurance

The blessed assurance
Resting upon Your word,
Gives us sinners the chance
To follow what we've heard.

We cherish and uphold
Every word You utter.
Whatever You once told
Is dear to the letter

For You're good and faithful
With love sure as the sun
But though You're merciful
Of Your word You change none.

With faith as deep and blind
We put our trust in You.
Peace of the soul we find,
Strength for the journey too.

So the sweet assurance
Keeping us at Your feet
Soothes souls in advance,
Foretaste of divine treats.

Were It Not

Were it not for Your Love,
O Lord, where would we be?
Were it not for Your love
That all around we see.

The sun would stop shining;
No more baths in its rays.
We'd be slowly dying,
Icy darkness always.

Were it not for Your Grace
Dear Lord, where would we be?
Just losing every race,
Crushed under sins truly

For weakened by the flesh
We'd never be aware
Of the enemy mesh
Keeping us well ensnared.

If not for Your Mercy
Drowning our failings,
Were it not for Mercy,
Father we'd be dying.

Always our nature
Robs us of divine Grace
But You never measure
The size of our disgrace.

So in Your Love, dear Lord,
Warm as the sun, we'll bathe.
From the infernal horde
Your children You will save.

Dear Father

Blessèd Father, Father dearest,
Father merciful, most holy,
Blessèd Father, Father dearest,
You who sustain our lives solely,

Loving Father, Father holy
Who with Your love, carry us through,
Of Your children, please hear the plea,
Spare us this plague, we beg of You.

To My Baby

What would we gain from it,
What would we benefit
On such moment as this
That we'd seal with a kiss?
Will it make us complete?
Say, what we'd gain from it?

They pulled our hands apart
But we did not lose heart.
Though they thought it was wrong
We kept the loving strong.
Why can't we, for our sake
His blessed word, partake?

We swore on that first day
To follow in His way.
We should before we dine,
Taste of His bread and wine
And secure in our chests
The love with which He bless'.

What would we gain from it
But weaken our spirits?
For sure we'd touch the sky
But not His heaven's high.
Will it make us complete
Or such blessing deplete?

From my mother,

First Kiss

A rose blossomed upon your lip,
Early fruit of a virgin love.
I felt your tenderness so deep
That it carried me high above.

Sweet fragrance of innocent years,
Unending source of joy divine,
If my heart's still fighting its fears,
You cause the chill within my spine.

Only silence surrounded us
When to my love you give your lip.
Oh how I wish I could adjust
And not tremble when my heart flip'.

I delight in this first moment
When full of love and heart pounding
We exchanged the kindred fragment
Of every ounce of that feeling.

Sweet ray of your very first dawn,
Keep your very first kiss of love
Deep in your heart. So that upon
It, shower blessings from above.

PS

First kiss my lip in vain want to lose you never.
Memory in my heart will keep you forever.

Once We Had

Once we had
Lots of years ahead of us,
Once we had
Teaching to make us pious,
Once we had
Will power to remain just
Once we had
Drives galore to be unjust
Once we had
Lots of time to readjust
Once we had…
But failed many times and plus
Till we had
Within us the Lord Jesus.

Peace And Love

Peace on Earth, peace to all men
Says to us the great "I AM".
Peace on Earth, peace to all men
And resounds the loud amen.

This peace the Lord gives to us,
Is fruit of divine mercy
For indeed the Lord Jesus
Gives so much for the journey.

This peace therefore, as I say,
Is a precursor of love.
It is always wished this way
So to mention peace and love.

Bathing in the peace divine
Then our hearts open to love.
On the face grace comes to shine,
His Kingdom falls from above.

Peace again to men on Earth,
Peace the Lord bestows freely
And the peace to love gives birth
For us to see God's glory.

From my Erjola

I Always Wonder

I always wonder what I would be
To be touched by an angel
To fly
To be free
To reach to the stars
To find a place
To look down and see
To be away from this cruel world
Letting out the girl I want to be.

I always wonder how would it feel
To swoop down on you
To travel deep within
To reach to your heart and find the key
To search for a safe place, my sadness
And sins to bury in.

I might not have the wings to fly
I might not have the key to your heart
But I still know how to reach the sky
I know how to keep love from falling apart.

I give my soul
To the one for whom my heart beats
Because I believe in true love
And in candles that forever stay lit.

Even when my world gives up on me
And everything looks like a dead end
I still get on my knees
And power to go on from God I lend.

And knowing that you are by my side,
It makes me believe
That I'm a sweet little angel
Sent from above with love to give.

Damned Sunrise

Here comes the sunrise and I'm still awake.
Here comes the sunrise and without a break
I remained counting the sheep in the dark,
Running unafraid of that poor dog bark.

Here comes the sunrise but this here my plight
Is caused by the thoughts I chewed up all night
For the sole reason I received a text;
I lost all reason and my sleep went next.

Here comes the sunrise, don't know if I should
Be happy or sad. My eyes I occlude,
Will attempt in vain to cover the dawn
But still the sunrays will undew my lawn.

So come you, sunrise, do what you do best,
With your bright sunrays paint over my nest.
With my weary mind, to stop I promise
To think of the one that I truly miss.

Sheer Unison

So much I often search simple words that climax.
Just as much I conclude that I should just relax
And let my pen dictate
Of my lyrics the fate
And what is in my chest
To come out at its best.

But in the midst of all surging from within me,
Though I harbor the thoughts of all that I don't see,
The essence of my rhyme
Always come out on time
On paper to reveal
The whatever I feel.

This the world will not grasp for it remains foreign
To the mysterious brook of lyrical domain.
A muse is after all
Not at beckons and call
But rather the mere source,
The font one should resource.

The concerted efforts exerted in silence
Mirror with symmetry all the time you dispense.
In music, harmony
Enthrones its melody.
Your muse inspiration
Reflects this sheer notion.

For she knows much better the way to set in awe
The public targeted, the one she long foresaw
To receive her message
That she kept in a cage
And now to set to light
Through pens rendered so bright.

For so often we search simple words that climax
But often we should wait till she sends us a fax
For then the pen less lame
Seems to be set aflame
And rides in unison
Blessed inspiration.

My Flat

*I wonder, I wonder,
I wonder, my baby,
When will you ever grace
My flat of your presence?*

*I wonder, I wonder,
My darling, please hurry,
My world upon its knees
Stifles in your absence.*

Your Heart

Like an ass led to market fair
With carrot stick up in the air
So relentlessly I reach for
Your heart that I so much adore.

Nothing derails me from my goal
So I press on, daring and bold,
All through the days and through the nights
With all my strength I hold on tight.

To me it favors do or die.
I'll move the earth and then the sky
To reach my precious carrot stick
So far yet so close to my beak.

Like an ass led with carrot stick,
Though I remain quiet and meek
I burn in the yearn for your love
And so I pray to God above.

For He alone give loving treats
To praying souls as He sees fit.
Though to the world it seems futile
I pray and wait in the meanwhile.

Like a toddle craving cookie
That way upon the shelf he'd see,
Relentlessly kisses and pouts
And overwhelms dad with no doubt

I beg and beg, then beg some more
For your heart I yearn so much for.
Since good things, be it soon or late
Nudge always those who pray and wait.

Daydream At The Gym

And for the life of me
I could not decipher
Was it coffee or tea
Maybe her thereafter.

But for the life of me,
Well tucked under her spell,
I could see bigamy
Being forever quell'.

She was the oasis
In the desert I see
So I welcome the bliss
All for the life of me.

If One Day

*If in your life one day
A good friend comes your way,
Remember He did say
He's here with us to stay.*

*If in your life one day
Your blue sky turns to gray,
Be strong don't go astray,
Think of heaven and pray.*

*If in your life one day
You meet her, don't delay.
Give thanks to Him, I say,
I'm still lonely today.*

*If in your life one day
Your soul He calls away,
Trust in Him, He did say:
"I am truth, life and way".*

Brand New

The lovely shade of pink and blue,
Reminder of love pure and true,
Cuts through the hearts of me and you,
Setting for us a brand-new stage.

These true colors never hand-made
And of scenes thus far never played,
That make all other colors fade,
Keeping us daily in His cage.

We never knew when it began
But gladly we followed the band,
Saddling safely the wagon stand
Leading us surely to the bliss.

All in life is bestowed for sure.
What befell us is blessing pure,
Souls to mercifully allure;
Tangible proof of His promise.

Soothed by His embrace we marvel
For on this journey we travel,
All stories slowly unravel
To gladly make all dreams come true.

Before an old computer,

> *Finally as it seems,*
> *In time, before I scream,*
> *I made it to the part*
> *Where I can safely start.*
>
> *I did not lose my hope,*
> *Kept steadily the scope*
> *Though at times it appear'*
> *I would pull off my ears.*
>
> *So here I am, I said,*
> *But why am delayed?*
> *No, I just discovered*
> *I have naught to offer.*

Dreamy Whisper

Amongst the clever fields of the creating Hand,
Pass the blazing shadows of a summer sunset.
They hover in the haze over blistering sand
Where often comes to rest the forgotten hornet.

Never a soft whisper, not even a clear thought,
Everything is dazzling with deafening silence.
And over this here land, where the angels have wrought,
Is left the silky drench of peaceful existence.

The whisper of instant, the shortest of them all,
Clings desperately to each and every passing wave.
And in the deep blue sea, over the seahorse stall,
You will forever miss what's whimsically paved.

Nowatimes

The brisk autumnal wind blowing
Over the meadows of your mind
Failed to rekindle the cuddling
Of yesterdays you left behind.

So tenderly you hold her hand,
Regurgitating tender thoughts
But sadly what she couldn't stand
Landed despite how hard she fought.

So you remained in her embrace
Hoping it'd be temporary
But the grimace upon her face
Revealed it was in no hurry.

But in the meanwhile of your eve
Where time erupts at lightning speed
Your heart explodes right on your sleeve
But leaves her lenity arid…

Nowatimes, a few years ago,
Each and every time autumn lands
The subtlety of her sorrow
Rests heavy on her harshness stand.

So peacefully, like summer brook,
You regain your seat of candor
Qualming softly the time it took
To regain your youthful ardor.